The Alcoholic Woman's Mad, Mad World
of Denial and Mind Games

The Alcoholic Woman's Mad, Mad World of Denial and Mind Games

By Bonnie-Jean Kimball

Hazelden
Always, the pioneer

First published, March, 1978

ISBN: 0-89486-048-8
Library of Congress Catalog Card Number: 77-94793
Printed in the United States of America

CONTENTS

INTRODUCTION

D enial as an integral part of the illness of alcoholism and other forms of chemical dependency or substance abuse is certainly not a new concept. The devastating effects of denial in regard to the woman who is suffering from a form of this illness (or dysfunction) have, however, received little attention. Much of the literature dealing with the woman who is alcoholic or drug dependent appears to be centered on questions. Why did she drink? What led her to this deviant behavior? What caused her to become alcoholic or addicted? There has also been some "fact finding" as to the extent of this problem area among women of different ages and backgrounds.

The questions may be interesting, but they are often beside the point in view of the fact that little is known about the etiology (cause) of the alcoholisms or drug dependencies. These types of surveys seem to be directed to this premise: "If we can tell her why she is doing what she is doing, she will stop it." This is misleading logic. Theories range from the idea that women have been captives of degrading sex role stereotyping to the suggestion that if they stayed occupied from birth to death with dolls, children and nurturing others, drug dependence would never hit them.

By looking squarely at the many levels of denial concerning women and chemical dependency in our culture, we can see and perhaps avoid many of the impediments to recovery and rehabilitation which prevent an accurate identification (diagnosis) of the problem. Denial plays a major part in the difficulty of reaching chemically dependent women all along the line and in every stratum of our society.

At the outset, I would like to stress that I believe in the illness concept of the alcoholisms. As long as there are hairs to split, people will be pulling at them, but in this small body of work, I can avoid redundancy by defining some terms at the outset. This is the definition from the American Medical Association:

> Alcoholism is an *illness* characterized by preoccupation with alcohol and loss of control over its consumption such as to lead usually to intoxification if drinking is begun; by *chronicity*; by progression; and by tendency toward *relapse*. It is typically associated with physical disability and impaired emotional, occupational and/or social adjustments as a direct consequence of persistent and excessive use[1] (Italics added).

What is Drug Dependence?

When speaking of "drug dependence" or "chemical dependency," I include that of the alcohol type. There are more similarities than differences. All are characterized by physical and/or psychic dependence.

Psychic dependence is the most important concept in understanding drug or chemical dependence. It is the common denominator in drug abuse. People can become dependent on a wide variety of chemical substances that produce central nervous system (CNS) effects ranging from stimulation to depression — thus the terms "uppers" and "downers." Despite their differences, all of these drugs have one effect in common: they are capable of creating in certain people a state of mind

---

[1]*Manual on Alcoholism* (Chicago: American Medical Association, 1967), p. 6.

that is termed "psychic dependence." To the user, psychic dependence means, "I *need* and must have that drug."

There are many routes to this condition, and many reasons for taking drugs. Psychic dependence manifests itself as the "felt need" of the individual in response to the effects of a specific drug. The strength of this attachment or felt need varies with the person and the drug.

Psychic dependence is the core of the problem, the heart of drug dependency. The user believes she must continue to take the drug. If a woman gets hooked on pep pills (amphetamines, speed, diet pills), she comes to feel she must continue ingesting that drug in order to do her best or to get through the day. That pill is vital to her well-being. The same degree of attachment is evident with dependence on alcohol or other depressants.

Is this in itself a type of denial? Yes. She can certainly *live* without the drug, but her "mind set" (which accounts for a portion of her drug dependent tenacity) demands that she continue "depending" on it for habitual states of being, mood modification, sensation or altered states of perception. Oftentimes the abuser has to feel "off center." What we might term a "normal" feeling state has become unbearable.

Users and abusers describe "physical dependence" on stimulants such as amphetamines. Nonusers insist there is no physical dependence on these substances. Those who have taken stimulants over a period of months or years continue to disagree. They are lost without "the rush" or the excess energy.

Test this for yourself with a stimulant such as coffee, tea or cola if you consistently drink one of these in fairly large amounts. By abstaining from it, you experience the "felt dependence." Abstain for a couple of weeks, and you will be able to sense physical differences. Persons who drink large amounts of coffee may experience headaches, leg cramps and a decided drop in energy when they give up drinking coffee for a significant period of time. They do not feel "like themselves." They become drowsy. They want to eat more. Caffeine was used as the principal laboratory stimulant in the time of Pavlov.

These are some physical manifestations you may experience during abstinence from stimulants. Imagine going through the remainder of your life without ever tasting coffee again — but with a twenty-four hour program! This is the prospect for a chemically dependent person insofar as alcohol or other mood-modifying drugs are concerned.

This brief discussion of the definition of alcoholism and the differences between psychic and physical dependence will serve as useful tools as I go on to examine the effects of denial on the alcoholic or drug dependent woman and those around her. In the limited confines of this book, it is my intention to show the overwhelming part denial plays in all areas of drug dependence and to illuminate some of the dimensions of denial. The discussion will help you to understand:

1. The resistance a woman has to giving up her drug(s) or admitting her dependence on them

2. The fact that the alcoholisms and chemical dependency are terminal illnesses if left unchecked

3. The repugnance felt by others toward labelling her "alcoholic" or "drug dependent"

4. The ways in which society hides the woman alcoholic or drug abuser until it is often too late for help to be effective

5. The confusion which surrounds the nature of drug dependence

6. The honest dilemma of the professionals to whom the woman often turns first for help or counsel

7. The blaming trap

8. The stigma surrounding these illnesses

9. The obvious ambivalence of our society toward drug taking.

10. The nature of "mind games"

11. The dynamics of denial at the core of family life

12. The need for education concerning the dynamics of denial

13. The hampering and delaying effects of the "symptom" theory

14. The misguided attempts of the medical profession to prescribe additional drugs to allay or relieve physical or other serious consequences of drug abuse

15. The attempt of clergypersons to offer help with other problems which usually cannot be solved until the drug taking is halted

16. The personal responsibility which the woman must assume for her recovery

17. The scope of *deprivation* felt by the addict or alcoholic when abstinence begins and for a varying time into recovery

18. The importance of intervention by those who see the condition for what it is and the subsequent use of leverage to get the woman into a program of rehabilitation and recovery

19. The role you take as a helper

20. The fact that husbands often abandon wives who have become alcoholic or drug dependent

21. The responsibility for their own recoveries of non-chemically dependent persons who have been associated with the illnesses

22. The preservation of denial on the part of the woman far into recovery and while she is attending A.A.

23. The sustaining nature of sobriety for an improved quality of life

24. The importance of regaining self-esteem through service to others

25. The fact that as long as the woman and/or those around her continue to *deny*, the battle against surrender and acceptance is raging and recovery is hampered.

EVIDENCE OF DENIAL

Once upon a time, there was a singer who happened to belong to the American Automobile Association. One day a friend asked innocently, "Do you belong to A.A.?" The singer was furious and made it QUITE clear her membership was in Triple A, not double A. Why was she so upset by this simple mistake?

Once upon a time, there was a college professor who taught in a small Texas town. She had to go to the county line to find a liquor store. On the way back home, she played "chicken" with her car, driving on the wrong side of the road and forcing oncoming traffic into the ditch. She could see no insanity in her actions. What is strange about this behavior?

A lady who had been in treatment for alcoholism went to live in a halfway house for women. Her behavior was bizarre. She roamed the house at night and wanted to do laundry at three in the morning. The staff knew she was not drinking alcohol, but her speech was slurred and incoherent. She often staggered when walking across the living room. The Resident Supervisor found a large assortment of pills hidden in the secret lower zipper pocket of her elegant alligator handbag. Why was this alcoholic not sober?

The druggist in a small town began to wonder why the little nun from a nearby convent bought so much mouthwash. He knew she was making purchases for the entire religious community, but he had never known them to need such large amounts of that particular item. The grocer could not understand why the nun bought several cartons of lemon and vanilla extract each week for the convent kitchen. Were the good sisters actually eating that much garlic and baking great quantities of pastry?

Once upon a time, there was a lovely lady who promised her

husband she would not drink during the Thanksgiving holiday. She heard him coming toward the kitchen while she was preparing the turkey, so she stuffed a vodka bottle into the bird and shoved the roaster into the oven. Later, when family and guests had assembled, they heard a large "Boom!" from the kitchen. Why is this story more tragic than funny?

The denial involved with alcoholism and chemical dependency is not a new story, and although it has certain humorous aspects, it is basically sad. No one has yet explored fully the depth and extent of the denial systems which alcoholic women develop. We do, however, have some idea as to who, how, what, when and where. (Can we forget "why" for the moment?)

The chemically dependent woman is the "who." "How" is any way at all that will shield her from exposure to the world and from herself. She and those around her join in a deception to protect what society considers her basic femininity and womanhood. "What" is alcoholism, drug dependence, pill addiction, chemical dependency, drug abuse or problem drinking. The illness is treatable, but it cannot be cured. The damage is often irreversible. Whole families are affected or "infected" by it, and few family members escape emotional or psychological damage. "When" is until the strong light of personal honesty breaks her denial system. "When" may be up until she is dead. "Where" is at any level of our society and at every age.

Denial of the illness is rampant in our society. We have no methods of prevention or intervention that are as strong or as sophisticated as the ways in which a woman and those around her deny her drug dependence. We have probably seen only the tip of the iceberg concerning the alcoholisms among women, and many people refuse to recognize even that.

Denial is a way of saying "no" to reality. Once a person is in the throes of drug dependency, the reality of the condition is overwhelming, not only to her, but to all persons in her "systems": familial, social, vocational and cultural.

To deny drug dependence is to disown that condition. Until the woman has had appropriate treatment for her needs and comes to know role models who can be accurately empathetic, it is almost impossible for her or those around her to *own* the fact of her drug dependence. This is so because her illness clutches her being with the stranglehold of death. Others are ashamed for her.

To deny drug dependence is also to refuse to accept what is true, to repudiate facts. Is the drug dependent woman alone in her attempt to do this? Of course not. Denial is an attitude that permeates society and becomes a way of life for the entire family of the drug dependent woman. They deceive themselves in the face of facts concerning the alcoholisms, chemical dependency, pill addiction and any other type of drug dependency. *No one* wants to admit that the problem exists, especially when it is a woman who is the victim of the illness. This is a sociocultural fact. It is an important part of the "why."

We recognize denial as an outstanding characteristic of the alcoholisms and drug dependency. Alcoholism hits the individual like an accusation, a wet sponge in the face or a load of bricks on the head. In the face of this assault, heard from within herself or from others, the alcoholic denies defensively that she has a problem. In the opinions of specialists in this vast area of alcohol and other drug problems, this is *not* much of a defense. It is so expected and time-worn that it has lost all credibility. It is the usual reaction. The alcoholic who does not deny her condition is a remarkable exception. A typical dialogue may go like this:

"You're an alcoholic."

"Oh no, I'm not. How dare you say such a thing?"

Then come the reasons for her excessive drinking or drug use. They range from "a weak back" to "a strange tropical disease" (even if she has never been farther south than Minnesota). Nerves, family pressures or vague allergies are also common excuses.

This strain of denial runs throughout the core of our society, perhaps our world. The more we learn about ourselves and other nations concerning alcoholism, the more similarities we see. A nun visiting from Ireland told me that she resents the fact that most of the monies earmarked for the alcoholisms in her country go into research, not toward helping the individual alcoholic in treatment or recovery. Besides that, only those who will do their research in Canada can receive funds! In her opinion, this represents a desire to avoid uncovering the rampant extent of alcoholism in Ireland itself. Such behavior offers a prime example of how society continues to search for the "why" instead of facing the problem squarely.

Our country has also done a remarkably good job of denying the alcoholisms and drug dependency among women. There are basic, understandable reasons for this. I would like to explore a few of these reasons and their results.

BEDTIME STORY

This is a scene enacted by an alcoholic woman, Martha, and her husband George. Martha finds George in the den absorbed in a book.

"What are you doing with *that* book, George?"

"Oh, it's something I picked up in the college library," answers George, trying to tuck the book out of sight.

"It's called *Understanding Alcoholism*," cries Martha, grabbing it away from him. "Why are you reading it? Are you insinuating *I'm* an alcoholic?"

"No, no! I was looking at it to help one of my students. One of the guy's parents seems to be having a problem."

"Well, I don't want that thing in this house!" yells Martha, throwing the book on the floor. "Get it out of my sight."

"Honey, you know you *may* be having a problem, too," George suggests quietly. "It seems you're drinking more and more lately. I wish you'd check it out with Dr. Fixit."

"Don't be ridiculous. I know what I am doing. Alcoholics drink because they have problems, and they're weak. I don't have any problems, and I have willpower. I do my work. I work just as hard as you. God knows, I need some relaxation when I get home at night. I have to *unwind*. Since when is that a crime? I see that you and the children are taken care of, don't I?"

"I still wish you'd check it out with Dr. Fixit, Martha. It wouldn't hurt to ask him."

"I'm not asking for your advice. What I do with *my* money is *my* business. Just because your mother doesn't approve of drinking you think everyone's an alcoholic. Everyone in *my* family knows how to drink. I know what I'm doing."

Visiting Doctor Fixit

But George has planted the seed of doubt and Martha goes to see Dr. Fixit.

"I've been terribly depressed lately, Doctor, and I'm nervous and jumpy at night. I'm never really feeling up to par. What's wrong with me? What do you think I should do?"

These are the symptoms thousands of women present to their doctors. Dr. Fixit cannot make a concrete diagnosis on the basis of such vague complaints. He tries to explore the situation.

"Are you working too hard, Martha? Are you trying to do too

much? I know you're holding a job *and* taking care of the house, George and the children."

"I suppose I am doing too much, Doctor. I've been pushing so hard these past few months. I don't seem to be able to settle down, and I can never get to sleep at night."

"Well, I can give you a prescription for something that will help you relax and get to sleep, but I suggest you cut down on work and your extra activities. Get some exercise if you can. Maybe you and George can get away for a vacation."

There are countless variations of this scenario. Some women go to their clergymen first, but the majority of them ask their doctors for help when they begin having dependency problems with alcohol or other drugs. They want relief for the unpleasant aftereffects of alcohol and other drugs.

Unfortunately, they present the wrong, or at least the most deceiving, symptoms. Their complaints are extremely non-specific. The doctor often compounds the original problem by prescribing a tranquilizer or medication for sleep. This is music to the ears of the alcoholic or drug abuser. It is the kind of "help" she can accept without fear of being asked to *give up* the drug on which she has become, or is growing, dependent.

The doctor feels he has provided a quick, acceptable solution for the "problem" his patient has. He believes her complaints do not have an organic basis. He may be completely unaware of incipient alcoholism or chemical dependency. If he suspects its presence, he might feel uncomfortable dealing with her and/or "it." The threat of alcoholism may strike too close to home, since the wives of doctors belong to a "high risk" alcoholism population (more about this later).

Women who are having problems with alcohol or other drugs know instinctively which symptoms to present to their doctors. Their enablers often support this form of "planned helplessness."

"Help me!" cries the woman alcoholic, but she omits mentioning the specific reason she needs help. She does not want to believe that her precious liquid medicine or prescription is a part of her real problem. As her enablers smother her cries for help, her physician plasters a vague overlay of pharmaceutical veneer on the growing problem of alcoholism or chemical dependency by prescribing medication for her.

In the beginning, she knows only that she needs someone who will listen to her talk about her problem. She hears a frightening inner voice saying, "Something is terribly wrong," but she dreads this message and tries to tune it out. When another family member underlines her fears by giving even the merest hint that there may be a vague "problem," she begins searching for a sympathetic listener who will support her. She must be able to say to her husband or her daughter or her father, "Yes, I have been to see the doctor." If the physician gives her a prescription, it bolsters her report.

"The doctor said I was overworked and tired," she complains. "He's afraid I'm going to have a nervous breakdown." This last bit is pure invention on her part. "He has given me a prescription so that I can sleep at night. I just haven't been able to get my rest. That's why I'm so nervous and uptight."

It may not be long before she realizes a need for another sounding board. Sometimes she turns to a clergyman.

She is looking for another sympathizer. She continues to avoid the fact that there is a growing problem with alcohol and/or other drugs.

Visiting Pastor Goodspeed

The visit to her clergyman, like the trip to her doctor, is oftentimes a return to "Big Daddy." She will say something like this:

"You know, Pastor Goodspeed, I haven't been myself

lately." Who has she been? "I'm not feeling well, and George and I just don't seem to have anything in common any more. We're not getting along. Even the children are aware of this."

"Well, Martha, what seems to be the underlying problem? Is it communication?"

"Yes, Pastor, we just can't communicate with each other at all. George doesn't seem to understand why I'm so tired. I'm working full-time, and I try to do everything at home. I'm giving so much to so many people — George, the children, everybody — I feel empty inside."

"Well, I haven't seen much of you lately, Martha, and you're not looking well at all. Have you been to see the doctor?"

"Oh yes! Dr. Fixit has given me a prescription. He thinks I'm on the verge of a nervous breakdown, but I know I'd do better if I just had someone to talk to." She begins to cry. "I honestly don't know what to do anymore. Would you be willing to do some pastoral counseling with George and me?"

"Well, perhaps. Tell me, how do you think George would feel about that?"

"I really don't know. As you said, Pastor Goodspeed, there hasn't been too much communication between us, but I could ask him if he'd be willing to come in for counseling sessions with you."

Now Martha has something to use for intimidating George. She can shut him up! She will tell him Pastor Goodspeed is concerned about her, that he feels George is not communicating with her and that he, too, is afraid she may have a nervous breakdown.

"Even Pastor Goodspeed says I'm not looking well."

Now Martha can put the burden on George to come for counseling sessions with Pastor Goodspeed. She is relatively sure George will never accept this idea, especially when she tells him the clergyman *really* wants to talk with him because he is such a poor communicator.

Martha is absolutely right in this assumption. George will resist pastoral counseling as if it were voluntary excess payments to the IRS.

Martha can then say she made the effort. She *tried* to arrange counseling for both of them. She has been to see her doctor. She has talked with her clergyman. She has done "all the right things."

The beautiful part of this for Martha is that no one has suggested she should stop drinking or using drugs. *The unmentionable problem has remained unmentioned.* Martha has enlisted new volunteers into her army of conspiracy.

Within a year, Martha has a battery of evasive answers for concerned questions from family and friends:

"Oh yes! I have this absolutely *marvelous* doctor. He is *so* understanding! He knows I'm nervous and that I have a terrible time getting to sleep at night. He has me on valium and another prescription for bedtime." (Her unspoken thought is, "And thank God he doesn't say anything about drinking or taking diet pills.")

Or:

"*Of course* I've talked it over with our minister. George and I have had some marital problems, you know. We attended a weekend on marital enhancement, and the leader said we'd have an easier time if only George would come in for regular counseling. But I'm getting so *much* out of counseling with Pastor Goodspeed. He's really helping me." (The unspoken line is, "And he has never said anything about drinking or taking pills.")

Or:

"Well, yes, I finally *had* to go to a psychiatrist. He is the *most* intelligent man I've ever met! He's helping me to understand my weak ego strength, and he has me on thorazine and elavil." (The submerged thought is, "And we don't have to talk about my drinking or taking the other pills.")

These unspoken thoughts and fears may be completely disguised in her mind. She may not be consciously thinking these things, but somewhere in the depths of her soul, she feels guilty about her drinking or drug taking. Nonetheless, she will fight with all her strength against being separated from her drugs. She believes that they alone are holding her together. She may also be convinced she is an inferior, weak, evil or crazy person, but she knows she *must* have the drugs in order to exist.

Somewhere deep inside every addict, there is a penitent waiting to be confronted. At another level, however, she is relieved because no one is forcing her to stop. Unconsciously she is pleading, "Come in here and help me find my way out. But not yet!"

WHY DELAY?

Why do women delay doing something positive about drug dependence? Why do significant others in their relationship systems aid and abet them in these delaying tactics?

The last thing a woman in our society wants to admit is that she is an alcoholic or drug dependent or an addict. We know the development of these illnesses is insidious. As a woman spends more and more time drunk or drugged, she loses sight of what is actually happening to her. She fails to realize that she is becoming irrevocably "hooked" on the drug(s) she is using. The deeper she sinks into her addiction, the more vehemently she will deny it. She knows that bearing the label of "alcoholic" or "addict" will shake her world and change it irrevocably. People stigmatize her far more than any other member of our society when she admits she cannot cope with alcohol or other drugs.

In addiction, greater than the social stigma for the woman is her fear of having "to make it" physically without a drug escape route. Drugs have become a way of life.

The reasons why a woman in our society responds this way are understandable, and they are many. Denial gets to be the name of the game, and everyone plays that game.

WHY DENIAL?

When other people agree to play the game of denial, they agree to insanity. To be rational is to be consistent with reality. Persons suffering from drug dependency of any type seldom qualify as rational; certainly not at the time of intervention, treatment or early recovery. Unfortunately, neither do their "significant others," but the latter have strong motivations for change.

The stronger the degree of drug dependence, the more deluded the person will be in the beginning. The deeper the well, the longer the climb out of it. Each addict or alcoholic exists in a world of denial, out of touch with the realities of life. Reality has become a bogey man.

Life for chemically dependent persons is a series of *mind games*. Because they live in this unreal, irrational world of denial and mind games, recovering chemically dependent persons in treatment were once thought to be inveterate liars and "con artists." As we come to know more about drug dependence and addiction, we view denial as an *integral* part of the illness. We tell women in treatment, "You're not *bad*, baby. You're just in love — with a drug."

SHAKE HANDS WITH DENIAL

It is going to be there, isn't it?

Those who work with alcoholics and other drug abusers are actively acquainted with denial and mind games. These games are usually apparent from the first day of intervention, but the ex-user identifies them only in the slow, undramatic process of recovery. It may take several years to unravel the skeins of denial, delusion and mind games. The tapestry of recovery is a long time in the weaving. It is seldom a pretty picture.

For women who are drug dependent, denial becomes a way of life. No ostrich ever buried its head in the sand as deeply as the woman in our society who is in the late or middle stages of the alcoholisms. She does not wear rose-colored glasses. She travels blind.

This woman rarely receives the benefit of early intervention. We are fortunate to identify her at any stage. Our cry has been, "Please call us! We cannot find you."

None of us is in the "judgment business." (Part of the genius of A.A. from its bare beginnings has been the nonjudgmental approach to sharing and helping.) In treatment centers, we are in the business of recognizing and identifying problems as well as creating impetus toward change. It would be ideal if we could avoid labels such as "alcoholic" or "heroin addict," but in the current stage of the art, we seldom do. "Tell me what to call it, and I'll tell you what not to feed it," characterizes our present position.

We need to remember, however, that labelling is part of the problem of denial. If a woman bears the label of "soprano," she may dearly wish she were a contralto, or she may ask to be differentiated as a special type of soprano. People react negatively to many types of labelling, and this is most certainly true if the label carries any adverse connotation in our society. (Compare soprano with alcoholic! I have).

The label *does* matter. It alters the perception of others as well as that of the "carrier." If a person earns (or receives) a doctorate, for example, society looks at that person with new respect. (The doctor of education sometimes asks to have "Dr." after his or her name in the telephone book!)

The reverse is true for an ex-offender, addict or alcoholic. Society punishes them and discriminates against them in a variety of ways (insurance, driving licenses, gun laws) despite the length of recovery or rehabilitation. Is it any wonder that denial is a built-in reaction to bias and discrimination?

STIGMA OF AN ENIGMA

The stigma factor cannot be ignored when we discuss the alcoholisms or chemical dependency. What is the nature of this stigma?

It is a general feeling about the illness itself. We talk today about the stigma lessening. We suggest that, "The stigma is not as great as it was." The fact that we mention this in these terms underlines the fact that the stigma still exists. It is there. It is real and palpable. We can hear it breathing in the public respirator.

If you doubt this, you can try announcing to friends, family and the world at large, "I am an alcoholic." People will receive your remarks in a way that makes it quite clear that denial and the stigma attached to the illness are alive and well and living throughout our society.

Near and dear ones will probably say, "Oh, no! That can't be possible. You've just had too many unfortunate problems lately, dear."

New acquaintances may answer, "Oh?" and give you an enigmatic look. If you report your illness on an application for a driving license, you will be in for even more interesting reactions.

When we look at the general sociocultural stigma, we must acknowledge a special onus placed on significant others who surround the chemically dependent woman. Husbands, parents, children, relatives and friends all suffer "guilt by association."

The illness reflects on the husband in many ways, at least in his own thinking. It says something about his role as protector, his sex role, and it has implications for his business or professional life. He may say to himself, "I made a mistake in choosing her. She's not fit to be the mother of my children," or, "She's no good." Others will say, "Dump her — quietly or otherwise."

What are some of the other negative connotations associated with excessive drinking in women? If it is "manly" to drink, it is certainly not "womanly." We have all heard the remark, "Hold your liquor like a man." A series of specific images and pictures center on the man in a drinking role. In reference to the woman, we hear phrases with a totally different connotation, such as "Daddy's little girl," "Drink like a lady," or "The hand that rocks the cradle should not hold the scotch bottle."

How does the stigma of alcoholism affect the parents of the addicted woman?

They may be loaded with guilt and ask themselves, "Did she get it from us? From me? What did we do wrong? Is it inherited? Is there a genetic flaw in our family? Is it physical or was it her upbringing? Where did we go wrong? What was unsuitable in our home environment?" These are questions for which there are few answers.

As for other family members, children ask themselves, "Are we causing Mother's problem because we're bad? Is Dad causing it? Do we have a rotten family or home life? What's wrong with us?"

What about significant others? When a concerned friend or relative calls an alcoholism information and referral agency, s/he usually prefaces the story or questions by insisting that the woman is definitely *not* an alcoholic. "She's not *that* bad." *They* would not want to be associated with anyone who is "*that* bad."

DEATH BY DEFAULT

How bad is "*that* bad"? How bad does it have to get before someone seeks help? How bad does the woman have to appear in the eyes of others and herself before there is intervention? Must she be half dead before anyone takes action to summon help?

Must we always wait for cirrhosis of the liver? Brain damage? Attempted suicide? This kind of thinking is a significant part of the reason women do not come into treatment until they *are* half dead. The majority of women in treatment centers are farther along the fatal swing of the disease pendulum than are men. They are often older and more likely to be abandoned. Their prospects do not augur well for recovery.

Again ask yourself, "Who wouldn't deny drug dependence — especially at first?" For the woman herself, the stigma is almost unbearable. She has broken a taboo. Biblical writings stress the significant role of woman as wife and mother. She is meant to help others, subjugating her own desires to those of her husband and children. When ministers first become involved in problems concerning a chemically dependent woman, they may find themselves at odds with their biblical tradition. They *are* in the judgment business, if only in their heads. Training in an alcoholism treatment setting or Clinical Pastoral Education may counteract some of this tradition, but it is not uncommon to scratch a male minister and find a male chauvinist lurking directly below the surface.

It is apparent that the woman is a victim of the well-known double standard. Society often sees drunkenness in a man as funny, or, in some cases, as with the skid row alcoholic, as pitiful. In a woman, alcoholism is not seen as just a disease. It is a *disgrace*.

As we look at denial and other mind games in the context of the woman who is drug dependent, we will examine two major points: the nature of the denial and those who contribute to it, as well as the implications for all phases of intervention, care, treatment, recovery and rehabilitation.

I have written elsewhere of the concept of a "total recovery program"[2] for a chemically dependent woman. The more aware that a woman and her helpers become of the alcoholic woman's mad, mad world of denial and mind games, the more realistic can be their approach to a period of recovery and rehabilitation.

---

[2] Bonnie-Jean Kimball, *The Woman Alcoholic and Her Total Recovery Program* (Center City, MN: Hazelden, 1976).

ROCKY ROADS
AND THORNY PATHS

Accepting the illness of chemical dependency as a lasting, irreversible condition is a long walk down the rocky road of recovery. A woman can begin this journey by taking the first step with a caring person, someone who will assist her on her walk up the thorny path of surrender. Denial blocks that path.

Denial is a special bugaboo for the chemically dependent woman. It occurs in our culture and in others. Exploration of the facts shows denial to be both obvious and deplorable. It is quite understandable to the A. A. member. If the alcoholic woman is hidden in the closet, those who love her are usually leaning against the door, helping to keep her captive in the addictive cycle.

Being in the recognition business means that we, as helpers, learn to recognize denial for what it is, an integral part of the illness. Other members of the relationship systems are caught up in various degrees of denial. Unfortunately, this is especially true when the chemically dependent person is a woman.

Why?

Members of her family network, members of her employment system and significant others usually minimize her drug problems. No one wants to call the woman s/he loves an alcoholic in the first place, and certainly no one wants to admit that her dependency is a lasting, irreversible condition. This can also be true with men who are chemically dependent, but minimizing is a more common pitfall for those concerned with the well-being of a woman and her eventual recovery.

Ask yourself, "Who denies drug dependence?"

The answer is, "Almost everyone."

Now ask yourself another question. "Who would *not* deny drug dependence? The alcoholisms? Chemical dependency?" Would *you* not deny it if you suspected that one of them was the cause of your living problems? I believe you would.

SAY IT ISN'T SO

Long into a woman's recovery from chemical dependency, she may be holding denial in a small corner of her mind. This reminds me of the old song, "Say It Isn't So." She will be continually watchful or will actively seek proof that her condition is temporary. One woman sought out many doctors for assurance that her liver damage was reversible. The purpose of the search, of course, was an "Open Sesame" to return to drinking.

This kernel of doubt has been with the woman since her diagnosis. "I don't believe I can't return to drinking or taking drugs," is the essence of this hold-out thinking. So long as this is with her, so long as she remains skeptical of the diagnosis, she is an easy victim for stimuli which will cause her to return to the use of alcohol or other drugs. This is the "Why am I the only one at the party who can't have a drink?" syndrome.

If she tries what is termed "The Great Experiment," she will learn again that she is powerless over alcohol and other drugs. It can be a quick or a slow learning process.

The stimuli for this kind of relapse include:

1. Periodic published reports that alcoholics can return to social drinking
2. Programs of "treatment centers" which purport "to teach" alcoholics to drink socially

3. Recreational use of other drugs such as marijuana
4. Repeated encouragement of relatives, friends or misguided counselors that she now has "control."

I have heard frequently about someone's "Uncle Henry," *the* alcoholic who returned to social drinking. I find it interesting that I have never MET an "Uncle Henry" of this type. Those who suggest that alcoholics can return to social drinking are usually nonchemically dependent persons. What have they to lose? Nothing. What have I at stake as a recovering alcoholic woman? My life. My selfhood. My everything.

VISTAS OF IGNORANCE

An aspect of chemical dependency which makes it difficult to understand comes under the heading, "Fear of the Unknown." If you are in a strange home and wish to go into the basement, you may open a door and then realize you do not know where to look for the light switch. Do you feel comfortable and secure in stepping forward? Of course not. There is a fear of the *unknown*.

This same fear exists in regard to chemical dependency or the alcoholisms. Nothing is more apparent here than our lack of definitive knowledge. Not only is it true that we do not know the cause, but we are equally ignorant of the point at which one becomes drug dependent. Specialists in the field have called this the "X factor" because so little is known about it. We are unable to name it. When does a person stop being a heavy drinker or user of drugs and become dependent on them? How do you determine that your mother, sister or wife is an alcoholic?

Although we do know some of the signs which suggest that a person has crossed the line, we do not know the point at which a given individual makes the transition. We understand a bit about physical and psychological dependence on drugs, but we have no idea *why* some people become victims of these conditions while others do not, even though their intake of alcohol and other drugs may be similar. Since none of the so-called "experts" can provide answers, we are faced with a vast wasteland of question marks.

This confusion offers support for *denial*. The woman who is diagnosed as chemically dependent can wail, "How can you say I'm an alcoholic when you don't know what caused it?" Professionals can point to this same unknown factor and insist that alcoholism is merely a symptom of an underlying problem. Family members can hedge accordingly and pray their loved one will miraculously escape the label of "alcoholic."

In addition to this honest quandary, we have the questionable advertising practices of the media: the Pain/Pleasure Sequence. "Do you have an ache? Are you feeling depressed? Are you having difficulty getting to sleep? Don't worry! Take something for it."

"This pill works faster than *that* pill."

"This medication will give you greater relief than that medication."

In some countries such as Japan, the Pain/Pleasure sequence in advertising is illegal, but in this country, it is not only legal, it is the basis for millions of dollars in advertising business. Magazines and newspapers barrage the public with advertisements for alcoholic beverages. These ads suggest that if you want to be really sophisticated, you will drink such and such a scotch. If you want to have a marvelous time with a handsome man, you will order *this* kind of drink, "made with our special vodka." The "Black Velvet Lady" of billboard fame appears to be glamorous, seductive and as desirable as the alcohol she advertises. At holiday time, beautiful, full-color ads for a variety of alcoholic beverages fill the magazines and newspapers. For some people, this "come hither" advertising is worse than a return to the Garden of Eden with the Apple Sequence.

We know that the majority of people see and hear these ads and have no ensuing difficulty. For the person who might become an alcoholic or for the person who has the potential for becoming drug dependent, however, this is an insidious, death-defying method of advertising.

At this time, we have no way of knowing in advance which person in ten will become addicted. Which woman is the potential pill popper? Who will overdose accidentally on pills and alcohol? Which alcoholic mother, after she has achieved sobriety, will try a tranquilizer for her "nerves" and find herself back in the squirrel cage of addiction? Which college girl will elect to take speed or diet pills to help her get that much-advertised, emaciated figure? Which one will become drug dependent?

The message that it is smart "to take something" to help nature conform to the demands of society is the siren's song to addiction for many women. It can also lead to a score of D.W.I.'s on the same highway whose billboards sing the siren song of social drug-taking. This message is at least partly responsible for the carnage on our highways.

THE CLOAK OF IMMUNITY

What is the attitude a woman adopts during the process of becoming chemically dependent? What is she thinking? How does denial grow in her mind?

At first, the chemically dependent person travels under the great cloak of immunity. "It can't happen to me," she insists. "I'm too intelligent. I'm too spiritually-minded. I'm too experienced. It will *never* occur in my life. I can stop whenever I want to stop. I have control. I'm in the driver's seat." (The next place she may be is in traffic court or the morgue.)

It happens! When it is established that a woman is chemically dependent (or alcoholic), the question she asks is, "What happened?" Then comes the whine, "Why me?"

She may continue this wail far along the recovery road unless she is brought to some kind of understanding concerning her addiction and the realities of recovery.

In a treatment setting, the chemically dependent woman will often be thinking or feeling at gut-level, "How did I get here? I wanted only to be less inhibited, part of the fun. What happened? Why must it end like this?" Perhaps she deluded herself into believing that she was only "making the unbearable bearable."

Her reasoning at this point has little validity. A major part of the problem is her basic denial of the illness. "I'm not *really* an alcoholic." (She may be drinking as much as a fifth a day or as little as "a few highballs and martinis." It is seldom a question of quantity. It is a part of the illness to seek out reasons for denial.)

The woman who has used medication, who has had prescriptions for pain, diet, relaxation, more energy, sleep, calming her nerves, going to the bathroom, not going to the bathroom, being less crazy, being more crazy, doing anything and everything will say, "I was *only* following the doctor's prescription." She will insist, "I had a prescription for that medicine. You know it's my *medicine*. Why is it such a big deal *now*?" She will conjure up an unbelievable array of rationalizations and excuses. These become her mind games.

In the beginning of care, it may seem to the pill abuser or

alcoholic that her treatment is actually punishment and that she is guiltless. Anything can become fuel for her fire of denial. She did indeed have a doctor's prescription. She did indeed drink with her husband. The fact that she abused or misused that prescription and also drank at other times is seldom apparent to her. These are facets of denial.

Women who become alcoholic often use alcohol in a facilitative manner: to quiet inhibitions, to appear "cool" or sociable, to sleep, to avoid or mitigate loneliness. When their liquid medicine turns on them, their questions are, "Why me? How did I get into this predicament? Why am I suddenly an outcast? Why am I put into treatment with this drug addict?"

These are not always questions the woman voices, but at a deep level, she does ask them. They are part of her denial system.

Unfortunately, she may *leave* treatment with this same denial system intact. "Denial System Still in Operation" or "DSSO" is often the message at the end of a treatment record. This indicates that the treatment team could not break through to the woman behind the denial system.

WOMEN AND "MIND GAMES"

What are "mind games?"

Both men and women who are chemically dependent engage in mind games. Mind games are unhealthy mental concepts which prevent recovery and may lead to relapse. The immediate defense that a woman employs is so mechanical and automatic that she cannot differentiate it from fact. We can observe in her just how mechanical a defense mechanism can be.

Mind games and defense mechanisms may grow from character defects. These include self-pity, resentments, perfectionism, grandiosity, self-centeredness, blaming, procrastination, jealousy and being a "worrywart." Mind games become as comfortable as they are habitual. A woman who believes she must always worry what others think about her (1) housekeeping, (2) grooming, (3) possessions, (4) children will feel more than a little vague uneasiness if she is convinced she must give up a harmfully perfectionistic mind game. Oftentimes this uneasiness is directly hooked into the payoff (for her worrywart perfectionistic mind game). The payoff is, "I'll have to take something (have a drink or pill) in order to keep my sanity." By working compulsively in a perfectionistic frenzy, she causes symptoms in herself, such as an aching back, and she can reward herself with a pain pill or an amphetamine. Yummy!

Old Tapes

Some mind games arise from "old tapes," which may come from ancient parental injunctions or commands. These "tapes" suggest that, "I *must* worry about my parents, money, my children, my weight and what others think of me in order to please Big Daddy or Big Momma." Women allow themselves to become overly concerned about parental injunctions far into so-called adult life. The chemically dependent woman has enormous difficulty giving up "old tapes" during recovery.

Other mind games may develop from a blind sense of rebellion against these same parental injunctions:

"I don't care what happens to me."

"I didn't ask to be born."

"I don't care how I look."

"People are no good."

"I won't go to church."

"I should get as much love as I think I need from whomever I want."

"No one should treat me this way."

"I'm better (or more intelligent) than other people."

"No one understands me."

"I'm too sensitive (or creative)."

"I've always been 'special.'"

"I don't know how to take care of a car."

"How can a woman alone manage all these financial matters?"

"I have always been sick. I am an invalid."

"The women in our family were never strong."

Who Plays?

All types of women play these mind games, including single women, married women with husbands and children, married women with husbands and no children (sometimes the "empty nest" syndrome), married women with children and no husbands (burden of being head of the household), widowed women with or without children, divorced women with or without children and lesbians who live alone or with others. Anyone can play. If we watch and listen, the mind games of women around us become readily apparent.

If a helper cannot relate to a particular type of woman or her games, it is better to refer the patient to a resource person or consultant. At times, a counselor or helper must be reminded, "You need *not* work with (help) anyone beyond your competence." Oftentimes, the best helper is another woman who has experienced chemical dependency and has played mind games of her own. When a person assists with a recovery, it is *essential* for her to understand or "get on to" the mind games the patient plays. Eventually, the patient herself must become aware of them if she is to recover. A knowledgeable counselor with the ability to be accurately empathetic will help her to do this.

Self-exploration is difficult when a woman is sober, clean, straight and free from alcohol and/or other drugs. It is *impossible* when the woman is drugged or drunk.

Eventually, the depth of her self-exploration can be indicative of whether or not she will experience recovery. She must reach certain insights about herself, but she can seldom do this alone. The helper can be pivotal in guiding her toward these insights.

In order to do this, it is important for the helper to listen for mind games and be sensitive to them. It is also important for the helper to refuse to play.

Mind games will keep a woman drunk. They can also cause her to relapse. Reaching the chemically dependent woman is more successful when the helper is fully aware of the vast repertoire of mind games. *Listening* for them is important. Pointing them out will be a waste of time until the woman is detoxified and "unconfused" enough to follow what is being said and to begin thinking for herself.

Even when this time comes, she will be resistant to looking at her mind games. What will she do? She will deny them, of course, either audibly or to herself.

This is usually honest denial. She is incapable of believing she uses defense mechanisms. That is how mechanical they become. She does not see or understand them. She is seldom able to give up her mind games in the treatment phase of the alcoholisms or chemical dependency. She may be jolted into realizing the possibility of their existence, but it takes a considerable amount of time to give them up. It requires slow, undramatic recovery time.

Denial in all areas is one of the chief symptoms of the alcoholisms. To the deluded, denial makes sense. It is an integral part of the illness which arises from the understandable confusion of all persons involved.

Types of Mind Games

One specific category of mind games could be called the standard "cop outs." Since there are as many different types of the alcoholisms and chemical dependence as there are types of orchids, this is a vast area. Cop outs can include minimizing, maximizing, blaming, references to O.K. times, places and accomplishments, age, drinks, sex and color.

Many women want to present an appearance of daintiness insofar as their consumption or usage is concerned, so they try to minimize it. They insist that, "I drank only *miniatures*," or "I took only what the doctor prescribed."

"I drink only on holidays."

"I take pills just when I'm in pain."

"I may have a few highballs in the evening."

"Maximizing" is often the mind game of the younger chemically dependent person. The "kid" who has been on a thousand or more "trips" with every kind of drug imaginable is maximizing. There is nothing she has not taken or done. She is a million years old and the biggest "head" in town.

Some women maximize or exaggerate the number of times they have been in jail, or the number of times they have been hurt, beaten or hospitalized. It is common for women of all ages to maximize their psychological, emotional, physical, familial or marital problems. "If you had all these problems, you'd drink, too."

The woman will make references to O.K. times, places and accomplishments to justify her behavior and illustrate that she is all right. She is not "that bad."

"I always have a clean house."

"I always have my work done on time."

"I am one of the most respected workers in our company. I never miss a day's work."

"I always get my husband's breakfast."

"My children are immaculate."

She is obviously trying to justify her drug use by insisting that she is carrying on a "normal" kind of life. Another name for this game is, "See What a Good Girl Am I!"

Other types of defense mechanisms or mind games include projection, repression, rationalization, euphoric recall and blackouts. The woman often uses different types of defense mechanisms or mind games to mask her loss of self-worth. She denies her feelings of inadequacy and self-hate and disguises her chronic self-loathing with grandiosity.

She attacks others. She may project her hateful feelings on them. She may be suspicious. She may actually be paranoid, and she certainly suffers from anxiety. You cannot expect honesty from her, because her feelings are not consistent with reality, and she is not rational.

ENABLERS ALL

When the woman is locked in denial, all persons in her systems will undoubtedly continue to support this denial to the death unless there is education for them. They do not want to call her an "alcoholic." If she is so diagnosed, family members and associates may go along with the diagnosis in order to stop the addictive cycle, but they refuse to see alcoholism as a lasting and irreversible condition. It does not appear to be a serious illness once the woman has begun to act something like her "real self" again.

Family members, parents, husbands and other concerned persons seldom realize that the addictive cycle can be set in motion again if the woman returns to alcohol and/or other drugs. Family members may become enablers. They can facilitate a relapse. This is one reason for educating families, husbands and significant others.

No woman wants to admit she is drug dependent. Those around her enter into a conspiracy to help her hide. They aid her in her feelings of secretiveness. Her loved ones come to believe that once she solves that *other* problem, she will not appear to be an alcoholic, a pill head or a drug addict. No one wants to see chemical dependency as a primary illness in its own right: a chronic, terminal illness. The woman is subject to relapse, an acknowledged part of the disease itself, but this is an additional puzzle to her enablers.

It is easy for counselors and other professionals in the field to be dissuaded into behaving and thinking in a way that supports the "non-illness" theory. If they encourage the chemically dependent woman in the idea that once she masters her character defects she will be a "perfect" person, they are leading her to believe a lie. "If I conquer all of my character defects I will no longer be an alcoholic." This is an equally devastating misconception.

By overcoming character defects, one does not erase all problems or the illness.

She remains chemically dependent. It is difficult for her and her enablers to understand that even if she becomes "perfect" in her behavior and feelings (which she will not), she will still be an alcoholic.

The self-pity, hostility and resentment a person feels are not the *cause* of alcoholism or chemical dependency. A woman does not end the *fact* of alcoholism or chemical dependency by ceasing the ingestion of alcoholic beverages and mood-modifying drugs. Abstinence does not erase the illness. This is also true of character defects. By improving behavior and attitudes and working to alter character defects, a woman can improve her mental and emotional health as well as her coping devices, but she does *not* end the fact of her chemically dependent condition.

Many times women will insist, "My family doesn't understand my alcoholism." Or, "My family doesn't know what it means to be chemically dependent."

The answer to this is simple. For those who help the chemically dependent person, for those who *are* chemically dependent, there is only a limited amount of knowledge concerning the disease. None of the so-called experts can explain the etiology of chemical dependency or the alcoholisms. Little is known. Emphasize this.

You must share the truth not only with the chemically dependent person, but also with those who are important to the support system of that person. It is necessary to be honest about the amount of knowledge which now exists. The accumulated understanding of the cause of chemical dependence is pitifully limited. Thanks to A.A., there is some knowledge concerning *recovery*.

It is wise to remind chemically dependent persons and those who want to help them that there are many more questions than answers in the area of chemical dependency. It is a good idea to counsel the chemically dependent person, "*You* do not completely understand your alcoholism, your chemical dependency or your drug addiction. If you understand even a few facts concerning your illness, that in itself will be a miracle. If your family does *not* understand, accept this. Do not depend on them for your recovery or rehabilitation. It is *your* responsibility. If they gain some understanding, if by becoming involved in Al-Anon, Alateen or other self-help groups, they are able to practice detachment and work on their own lives, rejoice in this fact. Do not expect from your family the understanding which no research person and no professional in the field can give you at this time."

The dynamics of recovery are especially mystifying to family members, no matter how good their intentions may be. It is extremely difficult for them to understand at a feeling level the need which the chemically dependent person has for ongoing support services as well as for abstinence. This includes understanding the importance of the A.A. Way of Life.

It was almost impossible for my family to appreciate why it was necessary for me to attend A.A. meetings following a year of sobriety. The idea of me mixing with "common drunks" from my hometown was especially repugnant to my father. After several years of recovery, it was his ambition for me to be able to drink with other members of our family. He wanted to see me as a successful college graduate only, an achiever who was free from any limitations of alcoholism or drug dependence. He wanted "my little problem" to be a part of the past, an illness through which I had passed. In his thinking, I had conquered my alcoholism. I had "willpower."

As I have said, families resist the idea of chemical dependency as a lasting and irreversible condition. At some future point in history, our knowledge of medicine or science may supply new answers for the chemically dependent person and significant others. That will be an interesting day.

At present, however, we must view drug dependency as a primary illness in its own right. It can be arrested but not cured. Those who suffer from the illness or have a loved one who is chemically dependent require support services from groups such as A.A., Al-Anon, Alateen and aftercare. People with problems who have gotten together to help one another are the best answer for ongoing abstinence, support and recovery. These groups and persons are vital to the recovery and rehabilitation of the woman as well as that of other family members.

A PRIMARY ILLNESS

Let us look for a minute at the greatest support a woman finds for her denial. What is the chief source of denial for everyone? Think about it. It is the belief that alcoholism or chemical dependency is merely a symptom of another problem, that it is not an illness in its own right.

"If Martha's marital problems are cleared up, she won't drink."

"If Martha's weak ego strength can be corrected, she won't take pills."

"If Martha's personality problems are straightened out, she'll no longer be an alcoholic."

Balderdash!

If a woman invests time, money, effort and emotion in other problems because she believes them to be the primary causes of her illness, it will set back her eventual diagnosis, recovery and rehabilitation, perhaps to the grave.

What are some of these other problems of which chemical dependency is considered a "symptom"? They may be emotional, psychological, personality, family or marital problems. These problems *may* in fact exist. They may be major areas of concern in the life of a woman, but until she understands and receives proper care and treatment for her chemical dependency problems, it is impossible to begin working to help the "whole person." Until she breaks the addictive cycle, it is a waste of time, effort and money to struggle with psychological problems. She cannot solve other difficulties when she is drunk or drugged. *First* the drug dependency, then the "whole person."

It is the goal of any comprehensive treatment or recovery

program to address the needs of the whole person. We are not treating the illness of the chemically dependent person if we do not encompass areas other than her drinking or drug taking pattern, but it is necessary for the affected person to make an exit from the addictive cycle before we can accomplish this. First Things First! (Where have you heard that?)

Many persons who are interested in what has become known as "women's lib" insist on helping the chemically dependent woman raise her level of "sex stereotyping awareness" and "personal identity."

These may be worthy goals. We must lay much groundwork in chemical dependency, however, before the woman is ready to work on these other areas. During a treatment period of any meaningful length (at least two months) the woman will receive assistance in recognizing additional goals for personal growth in recovery. She will develop change objectives. She will begin to recognize and order her goals while she is still in treatment, but the majority of this work takes place in aftercare.

Recognizing the alcoholisms, chemical dependency or drug dependency *first* and finding care and/or treatment for them is of vital importance. The woman will make little or no progress in other problem areas while she is still "using." A drugged, drunk or intoxicated woman cannot respond at any reasoning level to counsel for emotional, psychological, familial or marital problems. She will behave, act, respond and think as one might expect a drugged or drunken person to do.

PROFESSIONALS PLAY THE DENIAL GAME

Professionals often support the greatest source of denial (the "symptom theory") for the chemically dependent woman. Doctors want to prescribe for her. It is understandable that they wish to ease her pain and heal her with medication. This, however, merely causes the overlay of another chemical dependency problem.

We know most chemically dependent persons abuse medication. They do not take pills as doctors prescribe them. This can be involuntary abuse. The woman may lose count of the number of pills she has taken. If she is still drinking, she may not have a clear idea of what the doctor has said to her, his warnings or admonitions. She can seldom remember how much medication she has swallowed.

What about ministers? Many clergypersons want to heal through faith. There is perhaps nothing wrong with this approach after the woman has initiated a strong program of recovery. The strength of her spiritual program will be a pivotal point in this endeavor, but she must remember that no matter how strong her faith becomes, she will *remain* chemically dependent. Alcohol or other mood-altering drugs are her poison.

My abuse of alcohol and drugs centered around my performance in music, especially as a singer. Ministers of my acquaintance still ask me to sing solos in church. This is not possible for me. For example, when I read the audition schedule in the Sunday newspaper, my immediate and direct reaction from gut to mind is, "What would I have to take to audition?"

So long as this is my reaction, my real feeling about musical performance, I do not intend to jeopardize my beautiful, creative sobriety by attempting to sing. Countless times I have tried to make well-meaning ministers understand that at this point in my recovery, I will not chance public performance as a solo singer. One minister said, "Jesus is ready for you to sing, Bonnie." My answer was, "I am sure He is. I am also sure He does not want me stumbling around your choir loft drunk on Sunday."

As a recovering woman, it is *my* responsibility to point out my limitations. To well-meaning doctors, clergypersons and other professionals, I present the facts of my limitations as I understand them. A woman can learn that this is a part of the process of recovery in the community. She seldom understands her total responsibility in these matters while still in treatment or during her early exposure to A.A.

This realization occurs farther along the recovery road. As she overcomes her denial of personal responsibility, she will learn not to misplace this responsibility by giving it to doctors and others she has seen as "authority figures." No doctor will "put her on valium" if she refuses to take it. No other professional person or employer can push her beyond her limitations as she knows them.

Following treatment, it may be obvious to others that the woman needs a structured or semistructured environment to support and help her in understanding these limitations as well as her capabilities and talents. In the environment of a halfway house, skilled helpers can continue to remind her of these important aspects of recovery and growth.

Eventually, however, it is the responsibility of each chemically dependent person to help professionals understand the facts as they relate to her recovery. In the environment of the family or the halfway house, that recovery can mean a new lease on life for all.

WHO ELSE DENIES?

When we talk with groups who have been involved with helping to get women into care and/or treatment, we receive answers to this question that are not surprising. Most of our society denies alcoholism, but the answers do pinpoint certain specific persons who encourage the process.

Some of these include:

1. Courts — judges and lawyers —
   The aim here seems to be to get rid of this woman as quickly as possible. Her basic problem, alcohol or other drug dependence, is swept under the rug.

2. The social worker "system" —
   Persons involved in providing these services would rather designate the problem as psychological, emotional or familial. They can get lost in their advocacy roles.

3. Marital and alcoholism counselors —
   Not all counselors in these categories ignore drug dependence, but many do prefer to deal with other issues and ignore the primary illness of alcoholism or drug dependence insofar as the woman is concerned.

4. Sisters in a religious community —
   The fact of alcoholism is often completely unbelievable to some of these women. They feel they are "protecting" a Sister.

5. School system personnel —
   These people often see the "symptom bearer," the child, but they are unwilling to go to the source of the problem, the mother.

6. Policemen —
   All too often, the well-meaning patrolman merely gives a warning to the intoxicated woman driver. By doing so, he is enabling a drunken or drugged driver to add to the national carnage on our highways.

7. Employers —
   Many employers shield the woman and deny drug dependence. In doing this, they merely lengthen the drug-taking period as she progresses farther and farther in her illness.

8. Beauticians and cosmetologists —
   These professionals could act as a rich referral source if they were to become knowledgeable regarding women and chemical dependency.

9. Bartenders —
   The persons who provide this service believe they are extending sympathy to a woman customer when in fact they, too, are perpetuating her illness.

10. Drinking or drug-taking friends —
    Those who are themselves involved in pathological use of drugs are the last to point the finger. Someone might return the favor.

11. Community organizations of which she is a member —
    Any other explanation is more palatable than alcoholism. Her minimizing will fool many of those around her.

You can doubtless add other examples to this list. The number of deniers is legion.

WHO ESCAPES DENIAL?

Perhaps the persons who are least involved in the denial of chemical dependency or the alcoholisms are those nonchemically dependent persons who work with the affected person in treatment centers, agencies or in the home. The majority of these helpers understand the alcoholisms as an illness. They become comfortable working with chemically dependent persons. They have made a choice to serve or intervene in these complicated and difficult illnesses.

If you want to help a woman who is locked in the misery of addiction, you can join their ranks. It is not necessary that you have all the answers. It is perfectly all right to say, "I don't pretend to know all the answers, but I know where you can get help."

In the beginning, in early intervention, you may be like the small boy who pointed out that the emperor was not wearing clothes. You can be the one person who interrupts denial by insisting to a woman that there is a problem and she *can* find help.

UNDERSTANDING ABSTINENCE

In order to facilitate recovery, it is important for the helpers, family and the individual to understand the dynamics of abstinence. There is considerable difficulty in this.

If you are a nonchemically dependent person, perhaps the best way to begin to understand is to elect abstinence yourself for a *significant period* of time. If you are a coffee drinker, giving up coffee for six months or a year will give you some understanding of what it is for the chemically dependent person to enter into a total recovery program — a twenty-four hour program of abstinence which can continue for the rest of her life. Understanding abstinence from an experiential basis is especially important for those persons who work with the alcoholic or chemically dependent person. Do not ask someone to do something you have never tried yourself!

We know that all individuals do not become psychologically and physically dependent on drugs. Psychological dependence for women, however, seems to be a strong threat. Some people presently believe that this dependence is the only type developed with such substances as the amphetamines. In other words, a woman does not become physically addicted to amphetamines, but she can develop a psychological dependence on them. This includes other stimulants. Is this true? Try it! For those who have taken stimulants for a significant period of time, there is an awareness of physical change when use ceases. The dependence *is* also psychological. Your mind set tells you, "I *need* this drug in order to function."

Once you stop using stimulants, however, there are definite physical reactions. You may feel lethargic, uncomfortable, tired, lacking energy or zip. You may try to compensate by overeating. Eventually, you must readjust your physical being to living without the accustomed stimulant.

With the use of major tranquilizers, physical dependence is also possible. Professionals working in the area of chemical dependency often dismiss this as being only psychological dependence. I ask those who have taken these drugs, "Is the major tranquilizer, the psychoactive mind drug, one which produces only psychological dependency?" The answer from many is, "No." (We bump our noses on denial at the level of the professionals once again.)

There is a type of physical dependence related to medication. It is physical dependence in the sense that the user becomes accustomed to physical changes which manifest themselves in the central nervous system. If you alter your perception of reality with a drug, and if you continue to ingest that drug for a significant period of time, you are going to *feel* and experience a difference when you stop using it. When a person uses major tranquilizers, for example, she may feel a lassitude, a relaxation and a loss of sex drive, all of which are absent in that person when she discontinues the mind drug.

The absence of major tranquilizers produces a great change as far as bodily reactions and functioning are concerned. This is usually overlooked by physicians. The effects are sufficient, however, to persuade the drug dependent person to continue "using."

We might call psychological dependence the "mad hatter syndrome." This is an irrational state in which what is unreal seems real and vice versa. At times, the person who is psychologically dependent on a drug will fear collapse without that particular drug. Physical change in the *absence* of the drug reinforces this belief.

To the drug, a woman cries, "I hate what you're doing to me, but I know I can't live without you. You are the most precious part of my life!" The love affair with drugs and the effects they produce is a personality-riveting phenomenon.

THE GREATEST GIFT OF LOVE

It might be well to point out at this time that chemically dependent persons who are forced into treatment or committed have as good a record of recovery as those who go voluntarily. Commitment can be the greatest act of love a significant other can perform.

By committing someone, you are risking her anger, her resentments, her hatred, but you are doing for her what she can't do for herself in the beginning. That risk will pay off. You may save the life of a loved one by committing her. Eventually, in recovery, she will come to understand what you did to help her, and she will lose her feelings of hostility and resentment. She will also have a chance to live again.

There is little value in counseling a person who is drunk or drugged. If you are the one who has your reasoning faculties in working order, you are the one who must act rationally.

If you wonder whether or not a person needs your help, it is well to measure the intent or predictability of her drug use. One question can help you decide whether or not a person needs assistance: "Is her drug use sometimes different from what she intended it to be and is her behavior (after drinking or using drugs) appropriate to her responsibilities?" (You might ask yourself the same question concerning your own drug use and behavior!)

With this question, you can establish whether or not the pattern of usage is pathological or unhealthy. It measures intent or predictability.

Do not be confused by the mind games a chemically dependent woman plays. Do not expect her *to reason.* You need to see beyond her mind games to get at the pattern of drug use or abuse. Let your gut feelings be your guide. Many well-meaning helpers do not intervene as early as they might. They are often fooled into thinking the person will do something for herself. This is seldom the case.

YOU AS THE HELPER

The drugged or chemically dependent woman does not distinguish reality from illusion. She believes her own mind games. She cannot see that they exist as games or understand them, for they have become a way of life. She cannot recognize them while she is involved in drug taking or drinking, nor will she be able to understand them for some time into recovery.

What is unreal seems real, and what is real seems unreal. You can help her only if *you* are rational.

The alcoholisms are indeed baffling. The illness is progressive, irreversible and insidious, *but* treatable. A helper must focus her attention on getting the person into A.A., counseling or treatment for chemical dependency. It is perfectly all right for family members and other would-be helpers to say, "I don't know all the answers, but I know where you can find help."

For some helpers, this may mean simply giving the woman the telephone number of an alcoholic information or referral agency. It may mean referring her to A.A. It may mean finding a counselor. People who have had similar problems will recognize the mind games of this woman. They are more in touch with reality than she. They will understand her defense mechanisms, and this will enable everyone to get down to the business of *recovery*.

Reasoning is usually useless. Never make a threat or advise a family member to threaten unless you are going to carry through. For example, a careful examination of local commitment laws and procedures must precede the declaration, "If you don't go voluntarily, I'll have you committed." The person who can be authorized to proceed with the commitment must be prepared to do so.

It is wise to find people who have leverage or can exert pressure. Often a teen-ager may be in this position, perhaps a young girl who can say to her mother, "I really wish you could stop drinking. I never want to bring anyone home while you are drunk, and I never know when that will be."

This may be the pressure necessary to help the woman take an honest, realistic look at how she appears to others, especially to those she loves.

By the time the pattern of usage becomes pathological, the woman herself will not make the change unaided. When in doubt, refer her to *help*.

Other family members will need recovery help, too, and as soon as possible. If they have not been constructively involved in the pretreatment phase, sow the seeds of recovery as soon as possible. Encourage them to enter groups which will enable them to deal with the problems of their recoveries. Al-Anon and Alateen are the two best self-help organizations for this kind of assistance because they follow the Twelve Steps of A.A. They also help the family member to detach and think of his/her recovery as separate from that of the chemically dependent woman.

ABANDONMENT

Let us say you are trying to help a woman who is potentially an alcoholic or drug dependent person. It is important that you understand as much as possible of what is involved. There are deep-seated feelings in society surrounding the woman who has broken such a firmly established taboo. Blame is apt to center directly on her. She herself feels the burden of blind guilt.

She knows that society expects her to think of others first. She "should be" involved in the roles of wife and mother. If she is alcoholic, people will call her self-indulgent, irresponsible and selfish. The prevailing attitude is, "If she performed her roles of wife, mother or housekeeper, she would not be doing *that*. She would not have the time or money to drink if she were behaving herself."

The chemically dependent woman is sensitive to these unspoken messages. They lower her opinion of herself and decrease the esteem which others feel for her. While women are growing up and as they try to respond to the demands and expectations of society, "shoulds" and "oughts" are much stronger for them than for men. Our sociocultural attitudes are especially stringent where women are concerned. We can hardly compare the drunken man, who is seen as "a barrel of laughs," to the drunken woman, who is "disgusting," "disgraceful" and yes, "morally suspect."

When a man becomes an alcoholic, friends, relatives and neighbors are apt to say, "Poor soul! That wife of his drove him to it." Or, "That poor husband! Who could live with a woman like that?"

The story is quite different if it is his wife who is alcoholic. Advice from friends and relatives suggests that he get rid of her. It is important that we face this fact: husbands often abandon wives who are diagnosed as alcoholic or drug dependent. The reverse is seldom true. Wives of chemically dependent men may learn to cherish their long-suffering or enabling roles. They do not leave their husbands unless there are unusual circumstances beyond that of the illness.

Abandonment for the alcoholic woman, however, becomes a fact of life. Those who are trying to intervene or help the woman must be aware of this circumstance. It is a possibility. When we are working with a patient, we must keep in mind, "If we cannot offer her something better in life than her drinking or drug taking, we should not interfere." (In all cases I have encountered, we *can* offer her something much better in terms of the quality of her life.)

It is well, however, to be aware of all the facts surrounding her recovery. Some women, such as wives of doctors, as I have noted previously, fall into the "high risk population" category. These women often enter their marriages with an unwritten contract which includes heavy social drinking. At the time the doctor realizes that success in his career may require limiting his social drinking, his wife enters the "empty nest" period. She has fewer and fewer responsibilities, and her intake of alcoholic beverages and pills may increase at an alarming rate.

We do not usually see this woman in treatment for alcoholism or chemical dependency until she has exhausted the psychiatric wards of private hospitals. Her alcoholism progresses far into the later stages of the illness. The doctor may place her in a treatment facility after he has made the decision to serve her with divorce papers.

Recognition of facts like these is essential for the helper, since the prognosis for recovery will be poor. The attempt of the wife of a doctor to regain the attention of her husband after treatment by returning to drinking is futile. She soon finds herself in the revolving door of treatment settings. She has been abandoned, and she is often one of the women we must watch die the slow death of alcoholism.

If we look at this situation, we realize how much work must be done with the family to avoid the abandonment of a chemically dependent woman. If this is to be even remotely possible, much effort and time must go into educating other family members, especially spouses. It is well to do this prior to or concomitantly with the treatment period of the woman.

In the pretreatment phase of intervention with the family, and specifically with the husband, encourage modification of attitudes. Advance the illness theory. This is important spade work which the understanding helper can do if s/he is aware of the dynamics of denial and abandonment. Ask the husband how he would respond if his wife had cancer, heart trouble or diabetes.

A husband may believe his wife is jeopardizing his business or professional position. It is easy for him to hear and heed the advice "to get rid of her." His instincts seem to suggest the same course of action. The helper who is *not* cognizant of these facts can do the chemically dependent woman a great disservice. The illness concept is important at this point.

The woman who finds herself facing divorce following treatment will have a difficult time entering a recovery program. If the courts label her "an unfit mother," she will have several strikes against her insofar as her chances for rehabilitation are concerned.

The stigma of the label "alcoholic" does not compare with that of "unfit mother." The *two* are an odious combination. An understanding, responsible helper can accomplish significant groundwork in the pretreatment phase in order to avoid this kind of disaster or setback.

MYTH OF EARLY INTERVENTION

At the present time you may hear talk about early intervention. That is what it is — talk. Early intervention is a myth. We seldom see the chemically dependent woman until the middle or late stages of her dependency.

Denial of truth is one of the major reasons for this. Through the people in her systems and the ambivalence of society, the chemically dependent woman has a complete network of denial.

All of society is ready to say, "That lovely mother, that sweet intelligent daughter, that attractive wife, *cannot* be an alcoholic, because . . . ." After that come the myths. She cannot be an alcoholic or pill addict because she is "too sensitive, too intelligent, too beautiful, too well-educated," and on and on and on.

What does this have to do with the ability or inclination of a woman to seek help?

First of all, she would be the *last* one to do it for herself. The process of denial causes her to ask for assistance late, sometimes too late, or never. The woman is ashamed and reluctant to seek answers. She dreads hearing the truth, and more than that, she cannot bear the idea of life without her drug. She also has a legitimate fear of being abandoned if she is diagnosed as an addict or an alcoholic.

The woman in the latter stages of chemical dependency is vaguely aware of the loss of her attractiveness. She is glad few outsiders see her. She wants to be isolated. She remains unrecognized and untreated. Later in the addictive cycle, she may be a recluse, emerging from her cave of conscience only when forced to do so in order to replenish her supply. She scurries back into the darkness of dependency.

As a result, the diagnosis of chemical dependency sometimes seems to be a shock to her. She is so completely wrapped in denial that she has blotted out her ability to reason. She, too, is a strong believer in the myths.

EFFECTIVE INTERVENTION

No one can reason with a practicing alcoholic or other chemically dependent person. They understand only *action*. Never threaten an alcoholic unless you mean to follow through with positive action steps. You can seldom frighten the chemically dependent woman into sobriety.

Action means strategy planning. How do you do this?

If you are planning the strategy of intervention, begin by determining your role. Who will you be? Are you an educator?

A counselor? A preacher? A fixer? A confessor? An enabler? Or are you merely a concerned person?

Avoid the "fixer" role. At some subliminal level, the professional counselor often falls into this trap, or an A.A. sponsor can mislead her/himself into believing that s/he is responsible for the recovery of the person. These unfortunate fixations add to the problems already present. They can retard recovery and rehabilitation. They may inhibit the woman from taking responsibility for herself.

The counselor in primary or intermediate treatment in a hospital or treatment setting may feel the burden of "fixing" the patient. This is a misspent effort. If the counselor assumes such a burden, s/he is playing into the total misunderstanding and denial of the real nature of chemical dependency or the alcoholisms, as well as recovery.

The urgency for "fixing" is apparent to the casual friend or concerned family member. Oftentimes the volunteer, lay worker or paraprofessional will encounter problems to which s/he has no answers. Admit your ignorance; it is the healthiest thing you can do for everyone concerned. You never have to play God.

It is important for the helper to say, "I don't know, but I know where you can get help." Prepare yourself with these answers. "People answers" are superior to "drug answers." All helpers must have resource persons to whom they can refer the chemically dependent woman. This can be *your* principal task.

It is of paramount importance for a counselor to realize, "I am not required to treat anyone who is beyond my competence."

This frees the counselor to make a referral or bring in a trained consultant who can help in an area that does in fact go beyond the expertise or competence of the person originally involved with the patient.

A certain nonchemically dependent psychiatrist works extremely well with men and women who are chemically dependent. A large portion of her working thesis emphasizes the superiority of "people answers" to "drug answers," and she places great stress on the importance of a "Higher Power" answer as superior to all others.

This woman appeals to the queen, or the best side, of every woman. She speaks to the child of God who is in each of us.

For those who claim it is a mistake to talk about a Higher Power, God or the spiritual part of the A.A., Al-Anon or Alateen Programs, I would point out the unmitigated success of this woman. She is "all soul." She herself provides an example or role model. Remember that A.A. says, "You may be the only copy of the Big Book anyone ever sees," and "Don't preach me a sermon. Show me one."

It is especially significant that this psychiatrist, this medical doctor, is not a chemically dependent person. She stresses the precepts of A.A., the values and basic principles. She understands the Program. She makes the Big Book the basis of much of her counsel. Her greatest attribute as a counselor of chemically dependent persons is her emphasis on spiritual change. I have seldom seen a recovering chemically dependent person whose sobriety I admire who has not undergone this change. Many of these people are in no way related to an organized religion, but they place their ultimate dependence on a Power greater than themselves.

COMMITMENT TO
A HIGHER POWER

Eventually you may ask the chemically dependent person, "To what have you committed your life?"

The period of beginning recovery is not too early to emphasize the importance of spiritual change. As with other facets of recovery, when the woman is able to think and reason again (when she is no longer toxic or confused), she can begin to assume the responsibility for making choices. She will discover the options that are open to her and the joy of alternatives. The drug dependent woman had lost freedom of choice prior to treatment and/or A.A. and recovery. Now she has options, choices and alternatives. She can return to the cafeteria of life.

In recovery, she will decide whether or not she truly wants to follow a program of abstinence. This is her decision. To do this she will need the help of a Higher Power, a Power greater than herself.

The woman will also decide whether or not she wishes to affiliate with A.A. or some other self-help group. She will choose types of aftercare, therapy and counseling. She can select the type of environment and work which are most conducive to her recovery program. Her choices seem limitless, especially by comparison with the prison of her drug world. The early treatment or identification process is not too soon to introduce the idea of these alternatives.

She has the sobering examples of the opposites: insanity, death (through suicide or other causes) or the misery of addiction. Any way she looks at it, recovery is "something better," a glorious opportunity.

Chemically dependent persons can speak to this point from

experience. They can illustrate the differences between being dry (putting the cork in the bottle) and being sober, which means experiencing the joy of recovery in the fellowship of A.A. and through the help of a Higher Power. They can describe a full, creative recovery as "Sobriety *Plus!*"

The majority of people, chemically dependent or otherwise, are "spiritual retards." This is a reality. In A.A., we work toward a higher level of maturity, becoming aware of the beauties of a spiritual dimension to a life fully celebrated on a twenty-four hour a day basis.

It is true that some recovering persons do not choose to affiliate with A.A. This is their right. Those who do not become part of A.A., however, miss the joy, fellowship and guidance which are available in that type of recovery program. A sterile, white-knuckle recovery has little to recommend it.

These are some of the choices for the recovering woman to consider. The introduction of a spiritual program need not be separate from the introduction of other ideas (such as A.A. and the illness concept) in the beginning stages of her treatment. Some counselors and clergypersons, unfortunately, are embarrassed or unwilling to mention God, although they know how important the God concept has been in the majority of "Sobriety Plus" recoveries.

Those who wish to "pussyfoot" in this area can continue to refer simply to a Higher Power or a "Power greater than ourselves." Some believe this Higher Power comes from love, the group or the A.A. Program itself. Many of those who enjoy a creative sobriety and reap the rewards of abstinence and a changed way of life believe in God as they understand Him.

Avoiding the importance of the spiritual program or refusing to admit the relevance of spiritual change constitutes another type of denial. There is no need to be apologetic concerning a belief in God. Such a course can weaken recovery.

THE "POLYPROBLEM" PERSON

The polydrug abuser is not at all unusual in our society. In a treatment setting, we see this person being helped to understand that she cannot put physical or psychological dependence on one or a combination of mood-altering drugs.

We also see the poly*problem* person in the treatment setting. Those who have psychological problems together with drug dependence are not unusual. It is certainly possible to have two conditions at the same time. This is the dandruff and athlete's foot syndrome.

When we are treating two problems, it is important to recognize that we must handle them separately. It only makes sense to treat drug dependence first so that the individual can reason and think.

Over a period of recovery time from drug dependence, many of the accompanying symptoms such as anxiety, nervousness, depression and so-called paranoia may not disappear. As long as the drinking or drug-taking continues, however, therapists can make no progress with the psychological problems or mood disorders of a person, obviously because the individual cannot think or reason clearly.

The drugged or drunken woman wastes countless hours, effort and money if she sits in the office of a psychiatrist or psychologist undergoing counseling for psychological or emotional problems. At the same time, the other persons in the support system are confused and misled. They expect some good to come from this time, money and effort spent with a skilled professional. Unfortunately, they will see the chemically dependent woman as the one who is uncooperative. It will appear to be her fault that she does not respond to psychotherapy. No one can expect her to benefit fully from this counseling until she receives treatment for her chemical dependency.

By understanding the importance of first treating the drug dependency condition, you can avoid these repercussions. You will no longer blame the woman for her illness. She will avoid the personal distress of what she and others can only interpret as additional failure.

What about the woman who has a dual problem? In addition to dependence on alcohol and other drugs, she may suffer from deep-seated psychological problems, or she may be a lesbian. The woman who is a lesbian should not be treated for that aspect of her life — as if it were an illness — when she is in a chemical dependency treatment setting. Counselors should make her aware, however, of her need to deal with feelings about her lesbianism during recovery and in aftercare. The genius of A.A. is again apparent in the admonition, "First Things First."

FAMILY PROBLEMS

A separate and important area of denial lies with members of the family. All too often, they refuse or have great difficulty seeing the alcoholisms and drug dependency as family illnesses. They do not recognize that each person has an independent "recovery" or growth time upon which to embark.

The family ship will list dangerously if all hands do not become aware of the importance of this individual learning and growth component of recovery.

Oftentimes, when significant others attend a treatment center family program, they will be victims of the misconception that they are at the treatment center and in the program to give information concerning the chemically dependent person *only*. Such is not the case. It becomes of primal importance that each family member gains awareness of the harm that all concerned have suffered from these illnesses. It is often difficult to isolate the so-called "symptom bearer" in the family. Many times, this is the youngest child. This does not, however, mean that others have not suffered because of the destructive nature of these illnesses.

Take great care to help each individual member in the relationship system look at his/her recovery. It is equally important that these family members come to understand three major points:

1. The essence and practice of the A.A., Al-Anon or Alateen Program of recovery;
2. The difficulty of abstinence as a way of life, but on a twenty-four hour basis, there is hope with a total recovery program;
3. The importance of "giving it away to keep it," sharing our insights into A.A., Al-Anon or Alateen with a new member.

The phrase "a family illness" is all too often talk and is seldom accepted as a problem needing understanding and action.

POST A.A. DENIAL

Denial can continue well into recovery. Women who have been actively involved with A.A. for a number of years can indulge themselves in new forms of stubborn denial. They may refuse to admit the need for medical help in certain situations, many of which have to do with predictable changes in their lives and bodies.

Physiological changes in the life of a woman sometimes require the understanding and expertise of a doctor. Chemically dependent women may become so truly frightened of medication and doctors that they refuse to seek needed help. They expect and demand of the A.A. Program things which it cannot possibly do. These are often extremists who believe the A.A. Program can be a substitute for everything in life. This is asking the impossible. It is akin to the bear who bent over backward too far. This is overcompensation. By refusing competent medical help, these women are apt to risk relapse.

The steps will not change the hormonal balance of a woman, for example. In menopause, many women require medical assistance. In the case of hormone deficiency, a competent doctor can prescribe drugs that are *not* mood-altering which could save the woman endless hours of depression and associated misery. The recovering chemically dependent woman may even misunderstand influenza. Its symptoms may remind her all too vividly of her former hangovers.

A spiritual program of recovery can be only that. It is better not to think of it as a substitute for a full, creative sobriety in the community of God *and* man. Science also plays a part in our lives.

Doctors are also the best choice when a weight program is necessary. The competent doctor will provide a thorough physical examination and make recommendations for the well-being of the individual. A balanced diet of smaller servings and fewer calories is often the safest course of action. The doctor will indicate exercise when it is appropriate. Chemically dependent women must take the responsibility to refuse diet pills or shots. It is unwise for the woman in *early* recovery to attempt a diet unless it is medically supervised. The feelings of deprivation become too great, since there is a deep sense of it in abstinence.

A woman may be having problems connected with her sexual functioning. The assistance of a trained specialist is the only sane answer. Too often couples insist on turning only to the A.A. Program when special counseling in specific areas could bring much-needed improvements.

Spiritual life and growth can also enrich the A.A., Al-Anon and Alateen Programs. Many individuals find their way back to the religion of their choices after becoming active in A.A. Since the latter is not a program of religion but one of spiritual change, a return to the church of her choice can benefit the recovering chemically dependent person and her family as well.

Lastly, a most important area of denial arises if the woman hears piper's music enticing her to "return to social drinking." If she succumbs to this noxious nonsense, she can lose months or years out of her life, and perhaps life itself. By denying that her alcoholisms or drug dependence is a lasting and irreversible condition, she is inviting relapse with all its attendant misery and possible degradation.

RELAPSE AND SELF-ESTEEM

It is well to say more about relapse at this point. If we accept the alcoholisms, chemical dependency and pill addiction as illnesses, we must accept relapse as part of these illnesses. If a man has pneumonia, he is apt to cough. An alcoholic may drink again. By definition, the alcoholisms are characterized by relapse.

Some treat relapse as a disgrace. This can happen among professionals in the helping field. There is a feeling of failure. A.A. sponsors may also experience great disappointment when their "pigeons" are unable to fly right.

Philosophically, it is well to admit that mere mortals cannot take credit for the recovery success of another person, but in the face of relapse, it is difficult to remember the unspoken rules and rationales. When an addict returns to the needle, those involved with her recovery invariably feel a sense of sorrow *and* failure.

This understandable but rigid attitude encourages a decided misconception in the mind of a woman in the process of recovery. If she feels that she must "do it once and do it right" insofar as treatment is concerned, she will have strong feelings of failure and guilt in the event of relapse.

Looking at the total rehabilitation of the chemically dependent woman, we can see progress from the moment of intervention, recognition or emergency treatment. In the first stages, she comes to grips with her illness, and this can continue with or without interruptions through a long period of recovery. If the woman who drinks again or returns to drugs is penalized by censure, a road block is set up on her journey to continued recovery and rehabilitation.

Nothing could be more injurious to the well-being of a woman or to her total opportunity for a new Way of Life. Try to see the forest of rehabilitation despite the trees of progress and relapse. Do not expect perfection. Nothing is 100 percent. Adding a load of perfectionism or guilt to the recovering person can cause her to see herself not only as a failure but also as an inferior person. It will lower her self-esteem once again.

SUPPORT VERSUS RELAPSE

Refusing to admit the importance of aftercare is another example of denial. "I'll do it myself," said the Little Red Hen.

For those persons who have been in treatment, aftercare services provide a helpful bridge for a return to the realities of their recovery environments. Growth-centered programs and support groups for women are important during later periods of rehabilitation and personal development.

A recovery program for each family member is vital. It is also an enormous help if members of other systems (the vocational, social or professional) can understand what the chemically dependent family faces in terms of recovery. These systems include employers, friends and associates.

A woman cannot hinge her recovery on the understanding of others, however — not family members, employers *or* friends. If she herself understands the dynamics of drug dependence, it is a miracle. If even *one* other person actually understands her condition, it is a second miracle.

As you can see, both the lay public and professionals lack knowledge. There is no understanding as to the cause of the alcoholisms or chemical dependency. It is equally difficult for lay persons to understand that there is no "cure." No one knows the cause, and there is no cure. What a *void*!

With this lack of understanding comes a recurrent problem. People continue to exclaim, "Martha has been in the treatment center six weeks! She was out one week, and now she's drinking again! Why isn't she *cured*?"

The understanding that alcoholism is indeed a treatable illness, an illness that can be arrested but not cured, is difficult to impart. A woman seldom accepts these facts at a deep level in

the beginning. Sad experience with dangerous relapse becomes the stern teacher. This exemplifies another instance of
the denial of society and the attendant harm.

GUILT FROM "POTTY" TO "MAD"

It is exceedingly evident then, that denial exists on more than a
personal basis. Not only does the chemically dependent woman deny her condition, but so also her family, significant
others, professional "helpers" and society in general collude to
deny the fact of her chemical dependency. This can have serious overtones for the woman well into recovery.

Some of the reasons appear to be strongly entrenched in the
Judeo/Christian tradition and other religions of the world. A
large part of denial comes from *guilt*.

It is interesting that even while society laments the "breakdown of the family system," families seem to go on imparting
guilt as well today as they have for hundreds and hundreds of
years.

Like the poor, guilt is always with us. People *do* transmit it
effectively. It is difficult to give high standards and ethics to the
young. Trouble arises in keeping them free from harmful addic-
tions and dependencies, but there is no difficulty whatsoever in
implanting a firm sense of guilt in all, including the very young.
This guilt can become a lifelong straightjacket.

The reasons may be obvious in terms of commandments,
cardinal sins, original sin and all the other sin concepts. The

more fundamental a religion remains, the more guilt it seems to imprint on the soul.

And guilt is not restricted to the Judeo/Christian tradition. The precepts of Hinduism teach equally questionable "mind sets" in terms of such elements as spiritual withdrawal, which allows the brutalities of "untouchability" and serfdom to flourish. The idea of "karma" (paying for the sins of past lives) turns poverty into religious theater.[3] We in Western civilization are not alone with these unfortunate by-products of dogma.

Our own culture has hundreds of other types of "little sins" which we drum into children. These range from potty training, not eating sweets before meals, not saying "please" or "thank you" to the larger "sins" of commission or omission: getting caught outwitting the government, breaking rules on the job, speeding on the highway. In the attempt to order life, we implant tons of guilt-producing dictums.

The woman who has been diagnosed as an alcoholic or chemically dependent person has suffered in her self-esteem and in the esteem of others. Additional guilt will doubtless lead to regression and complete failure in the recovery process.

How deep is this guilt?

Part of the addictive cycle of pill-taking or the use of alcohol involves hiding the supply. The medication abuser may lock her pills in the closet, while alcoholic women sometimes turn to alcohol substitutes such as cough medicine. At other times, they use prescription medications.

This hiding is often a highly irrational process, especially if the woman lives alone. It exemplifies the extent to which guilt and shame become part of her obsession. Some alcoholics are called "kitchen sneaks." They try to drink in secret. They hide bottles and pills. They drink vanilla extract or cooking sherry. They are secretive and miserable. Their lives are ruled by guilt

---

[3] V. S. Naipaul, *India: A Wounded Civilization* (New York: Knopf, 1977).

which increases denial. The best expiation of guilt in the A.A. program may come from sharing with others and giving of ourselves through service to others.

WHAT TO DO?

It is obvious that our "guilty" way of life is not going to disappear from the culture in the foreseeable future. The human condition is more or less "stuck with it." Even understanding does not make it less powerful in the dynamics of thinking or behavior.

Are there any solutions as to how this applies to chemical dependency and the misery of the chemically dependent woman?

There are.

About forty years ago a group of alcoholics began working together. As their success in recovery grew, they stopped and looked at "what they had done right." They began to codify their practices and new Way of Life. From this came the book *Alcoholics Anonymous*. A.A. represents the best working system, the best practical approach to the problems of denial and recovery insofar as the individual and society are concerned.

The chemically dependent person can learn acceptance of problems. She can learn the pitfalls of "blaming." She will become aware that she is not unique. She can accept the best system of communication in the world, word of mouth, in dealing with her problem, her illness. She can learn through precepts of role modelling, from her sponsor and others in the group and the helping professions, "to stick with the winners."

"If she can do it, I can do it," is a sound premise for the beginnings of recovery. Another is, "Act as if." If you have trouble accepting faith rather than fear as a way of life, "act as if" you had faith. Miracles do happen!

By getting in touch with the teachings of Al-Anon and Alateen, other family members can begin to learn these same truths as they apply to their individual recoveries and to the illness itself. In concurrent learning, family members can begin to recover together, yet with detachment.

All can stop denying and begin accepting — accepting themselves and the illnesses of the alcoholisms, drug dependence or chemical dependency. They can take a new look at their lives and the total human condition.

The sharing and honesty of A.A. are fundamental in dealing with denial. As professionals — clergypersons, doctors, psychologists and psychiatrists — come to understand this simple yet demanding daily program or Way of Life better, they can stop complicating, denying and ascribing blame.

The dynamics of recovery demand time. There is no quick recovery and there is no cure for the alcoholisms. We can only arrest the disease and enter upon a new Way of Life.

Professionals and others who want "short cuts" will be sorely disappointed. Sponsors and counselors who want to claim successes as their own will remain aghast at the setbacks which beset the chemically dependent person in relapse. No one can "fix" anyone else. Finding a "Power greater than herself" to provide strength may prolong recovery and provide rehabilitation for the woman as she returns to her family and community.

QUALITY OF LIFE

Denial and mind games are part of the excess baggage of the chemically dependent woman. Eventually, she must divest herself of this dead weight, or the burden may threaten her very life.

You as the helper need to be aware of:

1. The fact of her denial
2. Her self-defeating mind games
3. The fact of support for both her denial and mind games at every level of society
4. Resource persons who can effect help toward recovery and rehabilitation
5. The need for intervention at your point of access.

Do not believe that YOU must have the solution. Do not look for a "cure" for this woman. Try to call upon those who may have leverage to get this suffering person into some form of help or treatment. Refuse to "buy into" her denial or play her mind games. Try to insist with love that there is help available and that she will avoid endless misery and possible insanity or death from drugs if she accepts help.

No human being can "fix" this woman. Eventually, she will learn to accept a bit of reality and responsibility for herself. This will grow. You, she and those around her must have patience. Ask for the assistance of a Power greater than all of us.

Urge significant others (family members and other concerned persons who have been touched by the course of the illness) to enter into recovery and growth programs for themselves. Al-Anon and Alateen are excellent.

The selfhood of the woman is at stake. By finding and calling upon the guidance of a Power greater than herself, miracles can begin happening, but even miracles often take a *long* time. Counselors and other recovering persons can encourage her in sobriety. She will learn that abstinence is not an end in itself, but a means to an end — to a better quality of life. She will be pressing on toward a higher level of maturity.

Eventually she can begin truly celebrating life and using her God-given talents and experience to reach out the right hand of fellowship to others. A spiritual change remains fresh only in the giving. The gifts of sanity, recovery, growth and service to others combine so that she can turn her battle scars into works of art.